NOT THE AUTHOR [illegible]

Russell Ash is the pseu[illegible] Europe's leading noble [illegible] 1954 and educated at Et[illegible]g. After a spell in the Hous[illegible], contributing to the invention of the laser, maser and faser and Diet Pepsi, and a stint as a stuntman (or possibly a stunt as a stintman), he turned his attention to an exhaustive study of the use of the verb, "to be", in early Provençal literature. This, his 40th bestseller and a potential Booker Prize winner, has been described as 'his tour de force', 'a masterpiece' and 'his biggest mistake so far'. He is married to a former actress and lives in a converted mill in Hertfordshire. They have three children and a labrador called Muffin.

POSSIBLY THE AUTHOR BLURB

Russell Ash was born in 1946 and educated at an establishment that kidded itself it was a Great Public School and at Durham University where he obtained an utterly useless degree in Anthropology and Geography. After discovering – mercifully early enough to escape – that a career as an Aviation Insurance Broker was not quite his cup of tea, he footled around in publishing and was as amazed as his mother to find himself a Director of one of Britain's leading publishing companies – a position he has since relinquished. He is the author of a number of fairly humorous articles in *Punch* and elsewhere as well as odd books on odder subjects, such as highwaymen, the Impressionists and Sir Lawrence Alma-Tadema (a painter whom many regard as the worst of all time). He was married once and has a very nice daughter. Among his other loves he lists Toblerone chocolate and Turnbull & Asser shirts. He detests smoking.

Acknowledgements

A portion of this book (parts of the Lonely Hearts section) was published in the November 1979 issue of OVER 21. I am grateful to the then editor, Audrey Slaughter, for recognising this seminal, in-depth, penetrating study for the masterpiece it undoubtedly was. The rest is unique to this book, but is very much the product of many enjoyable conversations with my friends, whom I would like to thank collectively. I am especially grateful to Christopher Wilson (William Hickey of the *Daily Express*), for his suggestions for some of the Press entries, to Jancis Robson (wine correspondent of the *Sunday Times*) for aiding and abetting my lampooning of her profession – and that of her husband, restauranteur Nick Lander – and to Sharon Klaff for her encouragement, ideas for medical entries and for introducing me to the supremely talented illustrator, Tony Escott. Barry Humphries kindly allowed himself to be distracted from writing a film script to read my draft text and made a number of comments that were meaningful, relevant and altogether helpful. My publisher and editor, Patrick Janson-Smith, deserves particular mention for his perception in commissioning the book and continued support and helpful advice during its evolution.

The Cynic's Dictionary

Russell Ash

Illustrated by Tony Escott

CORGI BOOKS

THE CYNIC'S DICTIONARY

A CORGI BOOK 0 552 99052 3

First publication in Great Britain

PRINTING HISTORY

Corgi edition published 1984

This book is set in 10/11 Century

Corgi Books are published by
Transworld Publishers Ltd.,
Century House, 61–63 Uxbridge Road,
Ealing, London W5 5SA

Made and printed in Great Britain by the
Guernsey Press Co. Ltd., Guernsey, Channel Islands.

Contents

Introduction

It was a day like many others.

I woke up, feeling 'one degree under', or what used to be described at my school as a 'general malaise'. My doctor tells me 'there's a lot of it about', but since neither of us know what 'it' is, his diagnosis is less than helpful.

I showered, using a soap proclaimed by its makers to be 'A Totally New Experience' that was guaranteed to make me 'Come Alive' – though it seemed just like The Usual Old Experience and I felt as unalive as before.

Breakfast – high in fibre and low in polyunsaturates – at least, I think it's that way round; either way, my cereal contained a miracle ingredient, ZX43B – or maybe I've got that wrong too and it doesn't contain a trace of ZX43B, which nine out of ten scientists agree is harmful, if not potentially lethal.

The radio weatherman told me there would be 'sunshine with scattered showers', which was somewhat at odds with the torrential rain I could see through the window. I glanced at the paper: MY NIGHT OF TERROR: A MOTHER'S AGONY and TUG-OF-LOVE DRUG QUEEN: RED KEN LASHES OUT looked intriguing. I opened a letter from my bank manager urging me to 'regularise my account', which I take to be a hint that I should stop spending more than I earn; also a generous 'Personal Invitation' that appeared to have been written personally by a computer offering me a set of 'Collectors' Medallions Celebrating the History of the Hat' and which I filed in my wastebasket.

To work: the train was 'unavoidably delayed', most

probably by a loony who unavoidably chucked himself on the line, or maybe the driver didn't turn up because he's got whatever it is that there's a lot of about, or perhaps he's a victim of the toxic effects of ZX43B. I decided in future to use the car – a recent purchase, it has little rust and was formerly the property of one lady driver (who, I have concluded, never learned to use the clutch).

At work (the offices of Bodger and Grout, Publishers to the Gentry), activity of a sort having resumed after an unpleasant period of 'industrial action' which appeared to have consisted entirely of industrial inaction. I wrote some blurb for books that I described variously as 'thought-provoking', 'a towering sage', 'mindboggling', 'perceptive', 'sumptuously bound' and 'lavishly illustrated'.

Called my girlfriend who I found through a Lonely Hearts ad ('Gorgeous, generous, warm-hearted, affectionate, etc.') and arranged to meet this evening.

Called estate agents: if all goes well with gorgeous, generous, etc. we'll be needing somewhere bigger. No offers yet, but their description of my tiny flat ('Magnificent, imposing bijou residence, close to all amenities in fashionable highly-sought-after locale') makes it sound like a mini version of Buckingham Palace, so it won't be long now.

To lunch at a charming little place near the office, where the amusing menu contains more adjectives than nouns, I settled for a 'mouthwateringly succulent prime steak lovingly prepared to the master chef's own recipe' which tasted like burnt old running shoe.

On the way back to the office, I stopped off at the travel agents to arrange my hols, but still undecided between 'luxuriously appointed villa in idyllic unspoilt location a stone's throw from the sea' and the 'adventure holiday of a lifetime' with other 'fun-loving 18-30s'.

Back at the office, I dictated a few letters in which I emphasised my gross inferiority in traditional style by referring to myself as 'humble', 'faithful' and the recipient's 'obedient servant'.

I skimmed the paper for inspiration for the evening:

perhaps an 'eagerly awaited prizewinning whacky romp' of a film or a 'theatrical tour de force', or maybe we'll stay in and take up the offer of 'another chance to see an acclaimed TV spectacular' with a 'glittering cast'.

I left the office early to catch the private view of works by a 'forceful, dynamic, organic, painterly artist', which was rubbish. To the pub for a swift pint of Molewart's Exceedingly Bizarre Real Ale, which another customer assured me is actually made from chemicals in huge concrete vats in Hartlepool. Shortly joined by gorgeous, generous, etc. and we settled for a tête-à-tête chez moi. The rest is none of your business, but suffice it to remark that our relationship is based on mutual respect, it is deeply meaningful, the earth moves and it was wonderful for me too darling, thank you very much.

However, I'm starting to get this feeling that my 'general malaise' is brought on by a growing and cynical sense that all around me there are people out to promote themselves or some product or service, or to make excuses for their failings. It's probably just me being paranoid, but on the offchance that there are others who share my belief, I thought it might be useful to compile a sort of guide through the minefield of doubletalk, euphemism and deception. Hence THE CYNIC'S DICTIONARY.

ADVERTISING

Adult	Filthy
Ask for written details	Unfortunately we are legally obliged to state this; the 'written details' explain in convoluted legalese that you will be quite legitimately ripped off – unless you are bright enough to understand them.
Assembled in an hour	Still a bodge-up after six hours and two crushed fingers.
At last!	Just what you've always wanted; you will be eternally grateful for this miracle of modern science – a toilet roll holder with a digital clock.
Better than ever	Indistinguishable from the old rubbish we've been describing as 'better than ever' for years.
Better value	Better than what?
Big! big!	Average size.
Biological (washing powder)	Containing chemicals and enzymes that dissolve all sorts of things – cotton, wool, man-made fibres, fingers.

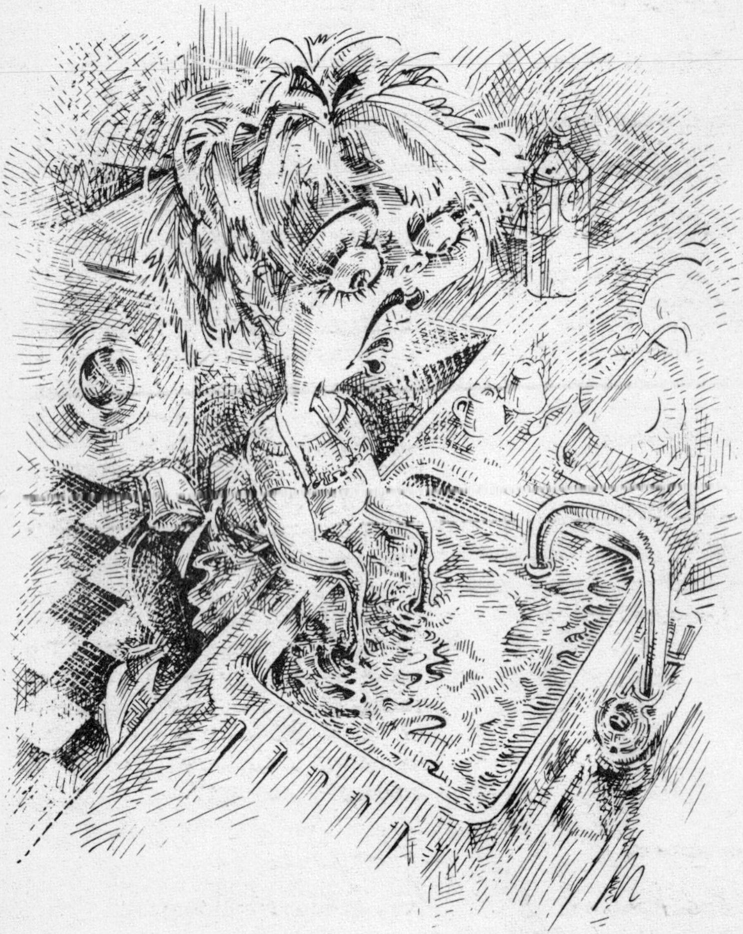

Biological (washing powder)

Biological stains	Urine, faeces, semen, perspiration, blood, sebum.
Child (as in 'A child could do it')	Probably a lot better than most adults.
Choice of colours	Choice of two colours.
Centre (as in 'Bedding Centre', 'Freezer Centre')	Shop.
Classic	Replica of old model.
Collectors' (as in medals, books, thimbles, etc.)	Implying that there will one day be other 'collectors' prepared to pay similarly inflated prices for worthless junk.
Come alive!	By slugging down one of our fizzy drinks or by taking a shower with a detergent smelling of pine, you will experience a miraculous resurrection.
Commemorative	Not unlike 'Collectors'; why anyone should actually want to own a medallion or a plate commemorating the death of King Ethelbert or the 150th anniversary of the invention of the Daguerreotype is a complete mystery.
Compact	Small.
Complex (as in 'Leisure Complex', 'Entertainment Complex')	Any group of buildings.
Crafted	Made.

Cuts the cost of . . .	But involves substantial initial spending.
Danger: Government Health Warning: Cigarettes can seriously damage your health.	Warning: Cigarettes can kill you – and you can't damage your health much more seriously than that.
Digital recording	More expensive and totally impossible for any human ear to distinguish from non-digital.
Discerning (traveller, clothes buyer, etc.)	Willing to pay a lot extra for not much more in the mistaken belief that he's getting a good deal.
Discover . . .	Buy . . .
Disposable	Cunningly designed so it can't be refilled, sharpened or cleaned, so you've no option but to shell out for another one.
Don't wait!	Buy now, regardless of the fact that the product will probably be improved and reduced to a tenth of the price, like electronic calculators in the 1970s.
Economy size	Small.
Elusive	Appealing to snobs.
Enviable	Ditto.
Ethnic	Made by exploited Bolivian Indians.
Event ('Carpet Event')	Sale.

Extra value

Exciting ('Exciting new fragrance', 'Exciting new cooker')	So long as you're easily excited, it's exciting.
Exclusive	You will be excluded from owning it or joining it only if you are not prepared to pay for it.
Executive (suit, briefcase, etc.)	Superficially respectable, but made of rapidly degradable materials, such as recycled cardboard covered with leather veneer — very uncomfortable if a suit.
Executive toy	Utterly useless item of desktop clutter, usually finished in chrome and matt black, that jiggles about annoyingly.
Extra value	A bit more at a higher price.
Feminine (products; see also under 'FASHION')	Relating to periods.
Fewer (colds, fillings)	Fewer than what? Fewer fillings than a person with 32 fillings?
Final offer!	Until a better one is forthcoming.
Formula X43	Prompting the question, 'whatever happened to A to W and 1 to 42?'
Fraction of the price	However, an unspecified fraction that could well be $\frac{97}{100}$ — an exciting 3% saving.

Guru/sage/seer/swami/yogi etc.

Functions, Many (calculators, video, watches)	Offering more confusing and quite useless facilities than anyone, other than a 10-year old child, would be remotely interested in. A corollary is that the most vital ones – such as the ability to adjust the time – are the most complex and the instructions, printed in 19 languages (including three not yet invented), are inadequately explained and are invariably mislaid.
Futuristic	A nonsense word; the future is never quite as it is imagined – whatever happened to all those monorails that were going to be whizzing round Piccadilly Circus, or those 'futuristic' costumes with little cloaks, silver boots and knickers worn outside stretch lurex one-piece suits that we were all going to be wearing on our day trips to the Moon?
Gentle; mild	Dilute; ineffective.
Giant size	Medium size.
Gracious living	The advertisers generously invite you to become a member of the aristocracy.
Guards against	Deodorants, air fresheners, etc., that cover up the smells.
Guru / sage / seer / swami / yogi, etc.	Peculiar Eastern mystic; usually either totally bald or heavily bearded, who talks a lot of gibberish and expects his followers to give him all their money.

Handsome (as in 'comes in a handsome presentation wallet') Superficially elegant, but made of cheap material.

Heirloom No longer essentially something you inherit; it now just means any sort of reproduction of 'heirloom quality'. It would be churlish, though, to suggest that your ancestor might have bequeathed you a piece of junk.

Heritage Similar to 'Heirloom'.

Homemaker Housewife; drudge.

Hours of fun for all the family Minutes of diversion for the person who bought it; the children will probably have more fun with the box.

Hundred-and-one-uses Only a couple of which might be employed by any normal person; or perhaps you *can* think of 101 uses for an anti-static clothes brush?

'I'm convinced' 'I have been paid to say, "I'm convinced" ' (that this is a major breakthrough, etc.).

Indispensable (gardening tool, kitchen gadget, etc.) Despite which, you — and most other normal people — have managed perfectly well without it for an entire lifetime.

Indulge; pamper yourself You are a greedy, over-rich self-centred pig; go and smother yourself with expensive creams and guzzle a pound of mint chocolates.

Investment	The only thing left to say about any over-priced and useless article.
Jumbo-sized	Packet of detergent the size of an elephant.
Kind (as in 'A new kind of . . .'	Rather like 'At last!'; something quite revolutionary, such as an instant custard powder that cures athlete's foot.
King-sized	For example, Edward VIII – 5ft 2ins in his socks.
Kwik konstruction	Kwiker kollapse.
Last word in (luxury, etc.)	Zymurgy, or maybe Zyrian; or possibly the last word until another comes along.
Leading (firm, shop, etc.)	Like 'Top' – a very crowded location.
Limited edition	Limited to the number we can sell.
Long-lasting	Doesn't quite wear out, disintegrate or get eaten immediately – just a few seconds later.
Lovable (doll)	If you love cold plastic, synthetic fibre hair, inane expressions and tatty clothes, it's lovable – but you're a pervert.
Lovingly crafted, polished, etc.	Buffed by machine; if you believe machines do anything with love, you should get together with the lovable doll fan.
Low tar (cigarettes)	Slightly less lethal.

Man-sized	Perhaps not surprisingly, not actually the size of a man, but a bit larger and twice the price of the regular kind.
Master (baker; butcher; plumber, etc.)	Any operative in these trades. Watchpoint: take care how you pronounce 'master baker'.
Medium size	Small.
MMMMMM!!!	Copywriter has run out of real words.
Modestly priced (but unspecified)	Outrageously expensive.
Monday (as in 'that Monday feeling')	Indistinguishable from the other six.
Name brand / Top name	Unless the product is normally sold in an unmarked brown paper bag, a somewhat unhelpful definition.
New!	Old! In New! packet.
Nine out of ten doctors, dentists, dog breeders, etc., agree . . .	BUT — one disagrees; perhaps he is more discriminating, or less easily bribed.
No nonsense (heavy duty power tools, chunky pens, etc.)	Weightlifting classes are advised before you start handling one; and if it drills or writes nonsense you have every reason to complain.
Over-sized	Although it sounds like a ghastly mistake — like Cyril Smith's suit worn by a midget — it's meant to suggest extra value.

No nonsense (heavy duty power tools, chunky pens, etc.)

Perhaps (also 'Possibly' and 'Probably') A non-commital way of implying that something is the finest, cheapest, or whatever, without risk of contradiction.

Period Old; the actual period must never be specified.

Personal hygiene Relating to the genitals.

Personal invitation Invitation to buy or subscribe to something mailed to you by a computer, along with the other four million people on the mailing list.

Personalized With initials.

Problem (skin, breath, etc.) Spotty; sweaty; smelly; loathsome.

Protection (as in 'personal protection') Either guards against (ie: covers up) horrid smells, or, possibly, a gun.

Quality Good quality? Mediocre quality? Lousy quality?

Quality controlled By a lazy slob with ½-inch pebble glasses.

Recycled Brown and speckled.

Rediscover Buy our product, go on our holiday, or whatever, in the mistaken belief that it will remind you of some forgotten pleasure.

Regularly (as in 'Use regularly') Use as much as possible so you'll have to buy more.

Relaxing Especially applied to substances designed to be dissolved in bath water; unless they contain vapor-

	izing soporifics or muscle relaxants that penetrate the skin, it is unclear how they can be effective.
Roguish	Aftershave purporting to contain pheromones or aphrodisiacs.
Routine (as in 'your beauty routine')	Conditioning process designed to make you feel insecure unless you make frequent sequential use of a wide range of pricey unguents; see also 'Regularly'.
Rugged	Not a million miles removed from 'No nonsense'; crude and unwieldy.
Sale must end Saturday!	So new one can start Sunday!
Satisfying (generally applied to cigarettes)	Providing the usual ephemeral narcotic effects.
Save!	Spend!
Scientific breakthrough.	There are breakthroughs and breakthroughs; a cure for cancer would be a breakthrough; a window cleaning aerosol that smells of nasturtiums is not.
Send no money	Send no money *now*; we will send you a bill for lots later.
Simply (assembled, glued together, etc.)	Precariously lashed together.
Smokeless	And heatless.
Sophisticated	High-priced rip-off.

Wet strength.

Special purchase	Cheap junk that gets round the law relating to 'sale' goods.
Standard size	Small.
Super absorbent	Until you stupidly attempt to convey it to a waste bin, whereupon it leaks profusely.
System	Incredibly expensive megawatt record player with wires trailing all around the room.
TV / Computer game	Insanely complex lump of hardware comprehensible only to small children who will tire of it at a rate proportional to its cost.
Ultimate	See 'Last word'
Unashamed luxury	Astonishingly, few consumers of luxury goods and services ever feel ashamed.
'We pride ourselves'	We complacently and fancifully imagine we are a cut above our competitors.
Wet strength	If you are very, very careful, it might not actually disintegrate.
Yes!	This is usually followed by such demands as 'Please accept my signed commitment to purchase 100 volumes of The World's Most Obscure Novels at £25.00 per volume' or 'Rush me a genuine ex-officer's anorak' (presumably the former property of a dishonourably discharged officer). Yes! therefore means, 'I am a sucker; I deserve to be put on your mailing list.'

Art Deco.

ART AND AUCTION

Antiqued / distressed	Lashed with chains, peppered with shotgun pellets and generally abused – sometimes by methods too disgusting to relate – to make a modern piece of furniture look ye olde.
Art Deco	Anything garishly coloured or angular made roughly between the wars – or even roughly made between the same.
Art Nouveau	Anything made at the end of the nineteenth century, give or take a few decades.
Attributed to . . .	A fake.
Award-winning design	Incestuous method whereby other designers, rather than those who are going to use a product or building, praise each other.
Conceptual	Unintelligible.
Empathy	Art critic running out of buzz words.
Enchanting	Small.
Evocative (as in 'evocative of the entire mood of the age', 'the spirit of High Victorian Symbolism', or whatever)	Worthwhile only if 'the entire mood of the age, etc.' is worth evoking.
Exquisite	Expensive.

Fantastic	Madly over-decorated – chairs made of stags' antlers, gilt-encrusted egg-cups, etc.
Happening	Dating from the 1960s; principally consisting of nude women covered in paint being dragged across canvases by German and Italian 'artists'.
Highly important	Providing highly important commission for auctioneers.
Homage to . . .	Rip-off of.
Impressive	Huge.
Interesting	I do not understand what the artist is trying to achieve.
Magnificent	Huge, and covered in precious metals and jewels.
Modern Art	A term of abuse.
Oneness	See 'Empathy'.
Organic	Containing convoluted shapes.
Painterly	This does have a specific meaning, but when it is used to mean 'what painters do' it becomes meaningless.
Perceptive	See 'Empathy'.
Plastic	See 'Empathy'.
Property of a Gentleman / Lady	Property of a dealer.
Spectacular	Monstrous.

Splendid	Quite expensive.
Tactile (painting)	Lumpy, paint-clogged hessian, to which a notice is attached telling you not to touch.
Technically adept	Sloshes the paint on OK, but hasn't anything worth expressing.
Totality	See 'Empathy'.
Very unusual	Very peculiar — such as a picture frame made of human hair or a steam-powered teatrolley.
Zeitgeist	See 'Evocative'.

BOOKS

Achievement	The bastard's delivered his manuscript at last!
Ambience	One of many words that say more about literary critics than literature.
'As told to' or 'with'	Ghosted by.
Authors / poems sought	Vanity publisher: you pay them to publish.
Award-winning	Winner of the Arnold Higginbottom Award for the Best First Novel about Scunthorpe.
Aware	Trendy.
Bestselling	Least worstselling book of the publishers' season.
Breathtaking	Preposterous plot that will have you believe that Freud was a Martian.
Brilliant	Average.
Committed	Fanatically biased.
Compassionate	Soppy.
Compelling / I could not put it down	Had I known what it was like, I might have been compelled not to have picked it up.
Complete book of . . .	The last word, until the next last word is published.
Creative	The product of an author's deranged mind.

Enthralling.

Devastating	One of those words that make you wonder whether you are reading a novel or an arms dealer's catalogue.
Emotive	See 'Ambience'.
Engrossing	See 'Compelling'.
Enthralling	Literally, 'enslaving'; if you want to be a book's slave, read it, see if I care.
Epic / Towering saga	Immensely long and tedious novel mentioning a few historical characters (Freud, Joyce, Wilde, etc.); often 'Sweeps across four continents'.
Erotic	Yet *another* detailed description of sex on a 'plane, with two Zulus or a consenting angora rabbit.
Evocative	See 'Ambience'.
Exhaustive	Exhausting.
Freewheeling	Unstructured.
Generational	Refers to me, my mum and my granny.
Honest	Cathartic.
Immortal	Fairy story, or tale of anthropomorphic rodents, beloved by parents and detested by kids.
Indictment	Vague accusation.
Intelligent	Pity, if you were expecting something infantile.

Intimate	Intrusive.
Irreverent	Rude.
Lavishly illustrated	Containing the fewest possible hackneyed old pictures to keep photographic costs, reproduction fees and printing bills to the bare minimum.
Literary	Intensely dull.
Masterpiece / tour de force	Latest novel.
Meaningful	See 'Ambience'.
Mesmeric	So unreadable that your eye will be transfixed to the page as you speculate on the hidden depth of meaning you have totally failed to plumb.
Mindboggling	Absurd plot set in Arizona desert and involving sex-change nuns, King Kong and a troupe of midgets.
Moving	See 'Honest'.
Outrageous	See 'Irreverent'.
Overwhelming	Long.
Panoramic	Failed attempt to encompass too much; as in most panoramas, everything at the edges is out of focus.
Passionate	See 'Committed'.
Penetrating survey	Revealing only as much as the

laws of libel allow.

Perceptive Not complete trash.

Picaresque Rip-off of *Tom Jones*.

Pictures, many never before reproduced And no wonder!

Prizewinning See 'Award-winning'.

Readable Simple language even a moron could cope with.

Relevant

Revelation See 'Penetrating survey'.

Riveting You will continue to read it in the erroneous belief that it will improve.

Searing Like 'Towering', but more violent.

Seminal A work so-described before it has been published has scarcely had a chance to become influential.

Sensitive See 'Honest'.

Shattering See 'Devastating'.

Significant Signifying what?

Steamy / sultry Pornographic.

Subtle Incomprehensible.

Sumptuous binding Over-decorated imitation leather surrounding paper that goes brown in a year and autodestructs in ten.

Sweeps across four continents	Author ran out of things to say and shifted the setting in a vain attempt to revitalize his Towering Saga.
Sympathetic	See 'Ambience'.
Thought-provoking	Unintelligible.
Thrilling	Containing a murder and a confusing plot involving spies.
Timely	Conveniently enough, written in time for us to publish it.
Touching story	See 'Honest'.
Towering	Overlong. A particularly *tall* story!
Unforgettable	Brain-washing.
Witty	Up-market funny.
Wry	Cynical and witty; puckish, droll and sardonic; not unlike this book.

BUSINESS

Amenity	Rubbish dump (except in estate agents' jargon, when it means 'shops').
Be that as it may (lawyer's phrase)	It is; I'm rumbled.
Business as usual	As long as you don't mind the concrete dust, pneumatic drills, muddy puddles, and bricks falling on your head.
Cashflow	Cash blockage.
Computer error	Human error in operating computer.
Consultant	Overpaid operative in ill-defined job; possibly redundant personnel who won't completely go away.
Demand (as in 'there's no demand for it')	You are the 37th person who's asked for it today . . .
Esteemed client	Utterly despised sucker.
Excellent working conditions	A desk, in an office, with a typewriter and a telephone; a tea-lady comes round twice a day.
Express (post)	One day faster than ordinary, if you're lucky; to Italy: totally meaningless.
Facility	Loan.
Five-figure salary	Closer to £10,000 than £99,999.

Scintillating.

Generous / fringe / other / usual benefits	15p a day luncheon vouchers.
Highly profitable	As yet unclosed tax loophole.
Humble and obedient servant	Highly superior and obstreperous overlord.
I am instructed by my client (law)	My lying no-good son-of-a-bitch client has perjured himself by telling me . . .
Immediate	Action in the next week or so.
In a meeting	Doesn't want to talk to you.
Life insurance	Death insurance.
Package	Any proposals in excess of one.
Position / situation	Job
Priority	Moderately urgent.
Property developer	Eyesore creator.
Rationalization	Trashing of personnel; cutting of services.
Regularize your account	Stop overdrawing without permission.
Trade fair	Gathering at which 'exhibitors' get drunk for a week and screw anything they can lay their hands on.
Urgent	Fairly urgent.

CARS

Advanced / car of the future	Car that looks entirely out of date when the future arrives; quite unsuited to the roads of today.
Average mileage	Average mileage for a long-distance truck.
Classic / marque	Self-indulgent, out of date and very expensive vehicle.
De luxe / Gran turismo	With extra stainless steel around the edges.
Economy test	'Test' during which a car is driven gingerly round a racetrack at a steady 50 mph in top gear, thereby suggesting it is capable of 56 miles per gallon; unless you customarily drive round racetracks at 50 mph your average will drop to 24 miles per gallon.
Enthusiast's car	Appealing to the sort of nut who likes to spend more time tinkering than driving.
Family car	As puked in by baby; seats munched by Labrador; bashed by bikes and prams; regularly not serviced by impoverished owner.
Fast	The property of a boy-racer.
Gleaming	Recent respray over old rust.
High performance	Incredibly expensive hunk of steel that overheats and oils up in traffic; costs more than the average house to buy, insure and

run, BUT is capable of a terrifying 200 mph.

Limit (as in description of car that 'performs to the limit') — Rev-counter set so the needle can't quite enter the red quadrant; at the limit of safety.

Low mileage — Less than 99,999 miles.

Many optional extras — Has wheels, battery and heater.

MoT — MoT Certificate expires next month.

Must be seen — I am a dealer and I am 100% confident of my being able to con you into buying it once I have you in my clutches.

Must sell — I have been bankrupted by running this gas-guzzler; girlfriend pregnant.

Needs attention — A wreck.

Never raced or rallied — Especially reassuring in the case of a three-wheeled Reliant.

No dealers — I am a dealer myself and am not 100% confident of my being able to con another dealer.

No rust — Some rust, but not too obvious.

One careful owner — Several careless ones; never driven in top two gears.

One lady owner — Batty old dame who used it only for short, cylinder-degrading, battery-wasting journeys, didn't know you had to put oil in it and never quite mastered that funny little pedal on the left.

Reluctant sale	Wife complaining about lack of comfort, expense, repeated breakdowns and neglect of her through weekends spent under bonnet by adolescent husband.
Slight crash damage	Eighteen inches shorter than it's supposed to be.
Some rust	Riddled with rust; more rust than metal.
Special	High-performance deathtrap, such as a Mini with a V-12 Jaguar engine; any car with anti-rollover bars, wide wheels, chequer tape, 'Sharon' decal on passenger side windscreen, more than two spotlights, fur seat-covers and megadecibel disco sound system.
Spoiler	Fibreglass attachment that spoils the appearance of a car without offering any significant advantage.
Tatty, A bit	Like a dustbin on wheels.
Taxed	Tax expires next month.
Thrifty	Modified to save 1% of fuel to the detriment of 20% performance.
12,000 mile service intervals	Runs badly after 4,000 miles, but if you're not too fussy will struggle on until 12,000 without the engine actually falling out.

Special.

Unrivalled performance	True only if it is the fastest car in the world.
Very clean	Immaculate body; engine worn out.

EDUCATION AND THE SOCIAL SERVICES

Able (school report)	Able to do the minimum and get away with it.
Assertive	Pushy; a bully.
Caring	Interfering.
Child of a broken home	Possibly a major contributing factor in its destruction.
Communicate	Talk.
Community relations	People of totally different cultural backgrounds and holding widely divergent views being urged to put up with each other in the hope that the poorer ones will stop mugging and robbing the richer ones.
Comprehensive (social service programme, school, etc.)	Incomprehensible.
Could do better	But won't, because he's a lazy little sod.
Deprived / disadvantaged / disturbed	Thug.
Educational toy	Elegant, but useless wooden object, or a mindbogglingly inane computerized game possessing the capacity only to educate a child to play other mindbogglingly inane computerized games.

Enrichment	Exposure to reggae, bizarre religious practices involving drugs and other alien cultural habits in the belief that it 'improves' one.
Frustration / insecurity / repression	The presumed rational explanation of irrational behaviour, such as vandalism and the mugging of old ladies.
Helpful	Teacher's pet.
Keen	But useless.
Maladjusted	Psychotic.
Media co-ordinator	Person who knows how to switch the video on.
Problem child	Bloody nuisance.
Progressive	Anarchic.
Resource centre	School.
Satisfactory progress	Mediocre.
Senior citizens	Relics; targets of violent abuse by junior citizens.
Shows promise	Which will, unfortunately, not be fulfilled.
Tummy ache (child complaining of)	Child does not wish to cooperate.
Underachiever	Totally useless.
Underprivileged	Poor.
Verbalize	Talk.
Workshop	Talkshop.

FASHION

Audacious / daring	Absurd.
Casual (especially 'casual hairstyle')	Taking three hours to achieve.
Cheeky / pert	Nymphette outfit.
Cleverly (as in 'Amanda's ensemble was cleverly made out of crushed Coke cans and plastic rubbish sacks')	Preposterously.
Conservative	Black velvet jacket.
Contour- / figure-hugging	Skin-tight.
Control (bra, corset, etc.)	Squeezes the fat bits in, or forces them into a position where they'll be less noticeable.
Creaseproof	Provided, of course, you don't actually wear it.
Designer	Emblazoned with someone else's non-removable name, or a motif depicting an amphibious creature. See also 'Exclusive'.
Devil-may-care / raffish / swashbuckling	Optional eyepatch, or trilby hat pulled down over one eye.
Elegant	Expensive.
Everyone will be wearing . . .	No one in their right mind will be wearing . . .

Exclusive	Expensive.
Eye-catching	Absurd and brightly coloured.
Feminine	Frilly.
Flattering	Attempts to disguise age, fat, etc.
Fun fur	Since it won't keep you warm, last long or stay in fashion, fun is about all you can get out of it.
Hand (sewn, finished, etc.)	Produced on a machine that can be programmed to replicate the unevenness of hand-produced work.
Heralding / signalling the return of . . .	When used to refer to such items of clothing as the bustle, stomacher or wimple, not to be taken very seriously.
High fashion	Ephemeral.
Individualistic	Hotchpotch.
Interpret	Rip-off design.
Little number	Price = big number.
Man made	Machine made.
Revival	Designer ran out of ideas.
Saucy	Matelot manqué.
Sexy	If worn by a funky, leggy, bra-less, black model, it's sexy; most other women will look frumpy.
Simple, uncluttered lines	Sacklike.

Striking	Nonsensical.
Stylish	Flared skirt.
Trendsetting	We hope it's trendsetting; if it isn't, we're lumbered with a warehouse full of the bloody things.
Understated elegance	Often used to describe the American view of 'English styling', for example, technicolor Madras cotton jacket worn with canary yellow golf trousers; tasteless.
Unusual use of fabric	Webbing underwear.
Whisper (as in 'a whisper of . . .')	Lace, always lace.
Young at heart, For the	Designed for mutton dressed as lamb.

FOOD AND DRINK

Acquired taste	Peculiar taste that is virtually impossible to acquire – unless you have absolutely no taste.
Baby (carrots, chicken, octopus, etc.)	Small.
Baby marrows	Courgettes, by any other name.
Bar-B-Q Flavor	Tasting of paraffin and charcoal.
Basket (as in 'Chicken in a basket')	Inexplicably served in a receptacle that is both difficult to eat out of and probably dangerously unhygienic.
Bed (as in 'Served on a bed of rice, lettuce, etc.)	Laid to rest.
Best / finest	Darn! Just when you were hoping for the worst.
Blend of	Mixture containing more of the cheap rubbish than the good stuff.
Bolognese / Milanese / Veneziana, etc.	Wallowing in tomato sauce.
Celebrated / famous / world-renowned	Boasting again.
Château	From France: anything from a real château to a tumbledown farmhouse.
Chef's own / special / special of the day	Yesterday's leftovers.

Choice of / selection of	Limited choice / selection of.
Coated with / cooked with / dash of / finished with / garnished with / served with / sprinkled with / topped with / tossed in, etc.	With.
Continental restaurant	Food with disguised origins — such as a restaurant with a French name and Spanish waiters serving Italian food.
Cooked to your choice / taste	Provided your choice / taste is run-of-the-mill.
Cottage	Factory made.
Country eggs	When did you last have an urban egg?
Country goodness	Synthesized in a factory.
Created / prepared by our chef	Made in bulk by chef's minions.
Crisp	Kept in a freezer.
Dew fresh / picked	Frozen.
Drinking well (wine described as)	Drinker enjoying himself.
Drinking wine	A wine to drink, as contrasted with one you might use to wash your car, strip paint or preserve biological specimens.

Farm fresh	Factory farm fresh.
Fast food	Fast indigestion; fast hustle out of restaurant resulting from lack of comfortable seating; fast return of hunger pangs.
Featherlight	Full of air.
Finger of	Not much of.
Fisherman's (pie, salad, etc.)	Fish.
Flamed	Immolated at your table.
For men	Allegedly lacking some substance that may or may not cause heart disease; pandering to women who are afraid their husbands may snuff it leaving them to pay the mortgage.
Fresh	Freshly removed from long-term deepfreeze; (eggs) not more than 27 weeks old.
Freshly cooked	Microwaved.
Garden (vegetables)	Lovingly tended by expert gardeners in a cottage garden; hand-picked ten minutes before they are served. You don't believe this, do you? After all I've told you?!!
Giant / King	Medium sized.
Hand-picked	Indistinguishable from foodstuffs picked by any other means.
Happy hour	Time when normally ridiculously overpriced mixtures of fruit

juices, tinting agents and minute quantities of alcohol are reduced to just steeply priced concoctions.

Hearty fare (pub grub) Bangers and mash, shepherd's pie and other stodge.

High toned (wine) Volatile; on the way out.

Home made Brewed in huge stainless steel vats, but cunningly made to look just like your mother used to ruin it. Possibly a genuine appellation, meaning, quite literally, 'made in a home' – unfortunately it's a home for sufferers from incurable and highly contagious tropical diseases.

Ice cream (British) Frozen animal fat blended with snow.

International cuisine Universal blandness.

Laced with Containing just enough to taste.

Lebanese style Served with shrapnel.

Mature (wine) Over the hill.

Mellow (wine) Excessively sweet.

Men prefer Men don't notice the difference.

Morsel Tiny bit of.

Mouthwatering Mouthwatering description; food dull.

Natural Raw; expensive.

Humble and obedient servant.

Old recipe	Totally updated by biochemists.
Pacific (prawns, etc.)	Pretty unlikely in Europe, unless frozen.
Pan-fried	Fried, astonishingly, in a frying pan – not, you will note, in an old wellie or a chamberpot.
Piquant	Takes your head off.
Ploughman's lunch	A hunk of French bread with a bit of butter and a few ounces of Cheddar, perhaps with such optional extras as a pickled onion; try ploughing ten acres on *that*.
Refreshing	Transiently thirstquenching.
Reserve (wine)	Meaningless, but no other description is legally permitted.
Rich (cakes)	Sickly.
Salad (as in 'Seafood salad')	Mishmash of odds and ends served with lettuce.
Scintillating	A culinary term apparently derived from physics, meaning the flashing that occurs when photons bash into each other; if it happens to your food it's probably radioactive and you'd be quite within your rights to send it back.
Seafood	Fish.
Sensational	Appealing to the senses of smell and taste – if not touch, sight and hearing; this is not actually too astonishing for something you can smell, taste, touch and see – and may even be crunchy.

Sizzling	Cooked on a red-hot slab of iron and served in a heated metal chafing dish; a synonym for 'burnt'.
Slimmers / slimline	Half the size and twice the price of the ordinary variety.
Soft (wine)	Must be consumed today; tomorrow will be too late.
Sparkling (drink)	Containing CO^2 under pressure; fart-inducing.
Special (beer)	Ordinary.
Specially selected for / bottled by	Cheap plonk trucked over in tankers and bottled here.
Succulent / tender	Somewhat superfluous adjectives if used in connection with meat, unless you seriously expected it to be as tough as old boots.
Surprise (as in 'Pineapple surprise')	Not much of a surprise once you have been tipped off that the dominant flavour is pineapple.
Tangy	Destroys 90% of all known tastebuds.
Tantalizing	Indefinable or alien taste, such as a banana that tastes of fish.
Thirstquenching	Transiently refreshing.
Traditional (as in 'Traditional Englyshe Fayre')	Traditionally cold, greasy and unpalatable.
Truffles	You must be kidding! Do you realize how much truffles cost?

Village Like 'Country'.

Vintage Bottled more than a day ago.

Vinted Made?

Wicked (dessert) Fattening — but that's never stopped you, has it, piggy?

Wild Tough.

Young See 'Baby'.

WINE

Although this wine has a certain aftertaste, it is amiable, ample, assertive and austere; its backtaste does not affect its balance; it is big, has body, is boisterous and has breeding; it is brisk, possesses charm, is clean-cut, close packed, crisp and both dancing and dazzling; it is dense, has depth, but is rather dumb; while easy to drink, it has edge, is elegant, elusive, enormous, fastidious and fat; it offers finesse and finish, but is firm, not too flabby, forward, fruity, full, generous, gentle or graceful; it is great and green, but has grip, is hard, huge, languorous and large-scale, with a length that is light-hearted, long, luminous, noble, piquant, profound, reserved, rich, robust, rounded, serious, shut up and silky; it has size and a smile, is soft and sturdy — if a trifle sulky, svelte, well-balanced and well proportioned. Unfortunately it tastes awful and gives me a headache, so I'll have a Perrier, thanks.

HOLIDAYS AND HOTELS

Adventure holiday You will be taken to a desert in an overcrowded elderly Landrover driven by a swarthy maniac who does 90 mph round precipitous mountain roads, accompanied by a bunch of aging 'funlovers'. You will be forced to cook inedible food over an open fire and to drink warm plonk until you are sick or fall over. There will be a sing-song round the fire, led by two hearty Australians who berate you for not knowing all 14 verses of the Anzac version of *Waltzing Matilda*. You will see a couple of Arabs with camels. They will permit you to photograph them only after you have paid them; they may even take American Express. Later, your bag, containing your money, passport and camera will be stolen at knifepoint in a bazaar. You will get dysentery and will be eaten alive by mosquitoes. If you play your cards right you could also be stung by a deadly scorpion, blown up in a 'disused' minefield or jailed for life as a suspected drug smuggler. The only attractive female in the party will become the property of one of the Aussies, while the other will eye you in a lascivious manner throughout the trip. The only other apparently unattached girl turns out to be a lesbian feminist who talks incessantly about the politics of menstruation. It will be hot and uncomfortable and will

	cost a fortune; you wish you were back home. Years later, however, you will recall it all as 'a marvellous experience'.
Breathtaking views	Hotel on the side of a mountain; swarms of asphyxiated tourists gasping for oxygen.
Complimentary (breakfast, wine)	Free, or apparently so; the cost is built into the price.
Exotic	Hot and primitive.
Fabulous	Either a nice holiday, or perhaps the real-life enactment of a fable – capture by Lilliputians, travel by magic carpet, attack by roc, etc. – though the travel insurance could set you back a bit.
Five minutes from the beach	If you happen to drive a Porsche 928 Turbo.
Fixed price	Excluding cover charge, service, VAT, etc.
Holiday of a lifetime	Because that's how long it'll take to pay for it.
Imagine (as in 'just imagine – miles of golden sand, carefree days, etc.')	Conjure it up in your imagination, because the reality is nothing like as enjoyable.
Non-stop fun	Gangs of drunken football supporters hurling each other into the swimming pool and raving at all-night discos.
Quaint	Completely unspoilt – at least, it was until the high-rise hotels were built.

Residents' lounge	Inhospitable room with a few old chairs and a black-and-white telly.
Stone's throw from the sea	If you happen to own a ballista.
Sunlovers	Pathological nudists.
Tourist class	Cheapest, most basic service.
Unforgettable (holiday)	Because the American Express bills keep coming to remind you.
Unspoilt	Except by the presence of a 900-room hotel.
Welcome	One free drink, possibly to the accompaniment of singers in grass skirts.

HOUSE AND HOME

Abundant vegetation	Wilderness garden.
Accent (as in 'the accent is on luxury')	Could be acute or even grave.
Adorable	Minute.
Air conditioning	In Britain, a device that noisily churns the same stale hot air round and round; not to be confused with the American equivalent that noisily turns the room into an icebox.
Architect designed	An experimental self-indulgence that failed; questionably an improvement on a house designed by a lion tamer.
Baronial style	Any description with 'style' in it is suspect; this one means it has a lot of sombre wood panelling, wrought ironwork and perhaps the odd moose head.
Bijou residence	So tiny that visitors ask you, "where are the other six dwarves?"
Borders of fashionable . . .	But actually in unfashionable . . .
Character	Bizarre character.
Charming	Laura Ashley wallpaper.
Convenient for trains	At the intersection of six main lines and backing on to an all-

	night goods shunting yard.
Deceptive	Not unlike Doctor Who's *Tardis*; looks tiny, but once you're inside it resembles a Mecca ballroom; unheatable.
Discreetly furnished	And what could be worse than indiscreet furniture that reveals all your secrets to the neighbours? A blabbermouth sofa is the pits.
Dream (house, kitchen, etc.)	Nightmare price.
Effect ('woodgrain effect', 'marble effect')	Plastic coated.
Elevated aspect	On high ground – or possibly on stilts.
Embassy (as in 'would suit Embassy')	More than £1,000,000; bugged.
Family house	More than one bedroom; possibly rambling and impossible to maintain or heat.
Garden flat	Dank basement.
Georgian	Old.
Gourmet kitchen	Filled with massive chopping blocks and huge knives hanging on the wall; also known as 'Abattoir' or 'Sweeny Todd style'.
Gracious	Old.
Highly recommended	Desperate to sell.

High tech	High price, low style.
Holiday home	House with the second best of everything, inadequately and tattily furnished and poorly heated.
Immaculate	Repainted and generally bodged up in order to flog it.
Imposing	Huge; resembling the house in *Psycho*.
Institutional use	Like 'Embassy', but without the bugs.
Interesting	Ludicrous; impractical; perhaps owned by a madman.
Intriguing	Like 'Interesting'; causes one to speculate on the mental health of the owner.
Landscaped gardens	Possibly O.K. if they were done by someone of the calibre of Capability Brown; on the other hand, if his cousin, Incompetence Smith, was involved, forget it.
Listed building	Listing building.
Luxuriously appointed	Gold plated taps.
Must be viewed	Same as 'Highly recommended'.
Needs redecoration	Needs shoring up with steel girders; anything with 'needs' in the description requires urgent and expensive attention.
Offers potential	A shambles.

Outstanding	Fabulously expensive.
Period	Old.
Picture window	A window you can look through — or possibly one with a reproduction of the Mona Lisa glued to it.
Pine	Any flimsy softwood.
Prestige address	E.g: c/o Buckingham Palace, London SW1.
Quaint	Falling down.
Queen sized (bed)	Normal size.
Realistically priced	Reduced, after failing to get unrealistic price.
Restrained	Fixtures and fittings related to 'Discreet'; decor that, all by itself, decided not to go over the top.
Scandinavian	Light-coloured polyurethaned wood, or woodlike substance; austere, boring.
Secluded	Miles from anywhere; spooky.
Selected (timber)	Containing 10% fewer knots and warps than unselected timber; four times the price.
Sought-after area	Inhabited by the same crowd for generations, so that few properties ever come on to the market.
Spacious	Vast; or, alternatively, of average size.
Studio flat	Miniscule; virtually everything

Unique.

	folds out of the wall — bed, table, cooker, bath, etc. All attempts to swing cats to test size result in feline fatalities.
Stunning views	Tower block.
Superior	Superior to what?
Swimming pool	In Britain, anything grander than a six-foot tub of icy stangnant water is described as a 'swimming pool'.
Tastefully decorated	Yes, but whose taste?
Townhouse	Interesting semantic shift: you'd expect a townhouse to be a house in a town, but nowadays they are invariably built in fields miles out of towns.
Ultra modern	Many useful high tech extras — voice activated garage doors, microwave toilet seat, masses of stainless steel and tinted glass.
Unique	Absurd; X-shaped rooms, bathroom in cellar, peat-fired central heating, arrowslit windows, piranha-filled moat, 5ft ceilings, painted matt black and dayglo throughout; formerly the property of an acidhead.
Unmodernized	Primitive.
Unusual	Unmortgageable.
Vanity unit	Washbasin.
Voluptuous	Former brothel.

LONELY HEARTS

Adventurous	Screws around.
Affection	Infection.
Affectionate lady sought	Shoolboy wants filthy-minded older woman with gigantic tits.
Afternoons free	Breakfast television presenter.
American	From New York: divorced Jewish psychotic. Los Angeles: Crazy; if in film or record business, snorts coke and talks rubbish. San Francisco: Gay. Anywhere between: Loud and boring.
Artist	Broke; smokes a lot of dope and talks a lot of nonsense about neo-cryptoquasi-Expressionism.
Arts, into The	When sex unavailable, willing to go to the Tate Gallery or see a film.
Attractive	Not attractive.
Average height	Average height for a pygmy.
Balding	Almost totally bald.
Bearded	See 'Hairy'.
Beautiful	Beautiful – and knows it.
Bisexual girls sought	Dirty old man wants to watch lesbians in action.
Blonde	Bleach-blonde; if male, possibly Nazi.

Boat owner	Part-owner of rotting canal narrowboat.
Bodybuilder	Gay, with Ortonian tendencies.
Bored	Boring.
Businessman	Old, fat and divorced; sells plastic E.T. puppets.
Buxom	Massive mammaries.
Caring relationship sought	Sponging, 100% supportive relationship demanded.
Car-owning	1958 Morris Minor-owning.
Civil engineer	Plays with Meccano.
Classy	Wears designer shoelaces.
Colour immaterial	Sexy black girl preferred.
Committed	Possessive.
Companionship	Easy lay.
Company Director, Rolls-Royce, Yacht, Rich, Penthouse, Lear Jet, Caribbean Island, etc.	Why does he have to advertise? Must have a serious problem: illegal perversion involving furry animals, 3ft 6ins tall, ex-Gestapo war criminal, mainlines Domestos, etc.
Continental	Arab.
Cosmopolitan	Foreign; much travelled and carrying many strange diseases; possibly the entire staff of a woman's magazine.
Country cottage	Run-down hovel without main

	services, miles from civilization; wants unpaid cook, housekeeper and bedmate.
Country walks, Interested in	Cheap outings, interested in.
Creative	Once went to pottery evening classes.
Cuddly	(See also 'Large') Man: bearded; drinks prodigious quantities of real ale. Woman: has six children; breast-feeds them in public.
Cultured	Has read *A Hundred Years of Solitude* – but doesn't understand it.
Cycling, Buddhist, camping, 'growth', longhaired, whole-foods, vegetarian, yoga, etc.	Sixties drop-out.
Cynic	Nice person; possibly the author of this book.
Dare you reply?	Don't.
Dark	Very dark.
Debonair	Lounge lizard.
Deep relationship	Deep-throat relationship.
Depth	What do you think?
Dining, Interested in	Man: makes obscene passes at meal table, gets paralytically drunk, throws up in his partner's

	lap and fails to perform – thank God. Woman: see 'Large'.
Discreet	Married.
Discreet gay	Top rank civil servant.
Divorced	Separated; may get divorced one day, but too disorganized at present.
Domesticity, Into	Nostalgic yearning for Ovalteenie père lifestyle.
Drives Porsche	Garage mechanic; swipes Porsche when boss away.
Dynamic	Space cadet; hyperthyroid.
Eating out, Likes	Possibly genuine gourmand; alternatively, cunnilingus-obsessive.
Eccentric	Strange; possibly homicidal.
Eclectic tastes	Devotee of an odd range of pursuits, the compatible matching of which is virtually statistically impossible, such as Mozart, hang-gliding and cannibalism, or laser technology, the cabbala and rubber fetishism, or – even more remotely – Bogart movies, the Arts and Crafts Movement and smoked salmon. What! You mean you're interested in them too? But this is amazing! Call me immediately c/o my publishers – reverse the charges if you like; see you on Thursday about 8.00 at L'Escargot, O.K.?

Friendly.

Educated — African.

Energetic — A sexual athlete; have an electrocardiogram test before you meet.

Ex-model — Former hooker.

Explore new horizons / dimensions — Horizons are notoriously difficult to explore as they have an irritating habit of moving away from you; dimensions aren't that easy either unless you have a *Tardis*.

Extrovert — Manic.

Eyes, Beautiful — Remainder vile.

Feminist — Horrendously hairy armpits, boiler suit and green combat boots; will drag you off to The Lesbian Marionette Theatre of Prague when you really wanted to see *Emmannuelle meets the Danish wife-swoppers*. Serves you right for being a horrid chauvinist, though.

Films, Interested in — Talks ad nauseam about obscure animated Peruvian anarchist movies; flatly refuses to see *Emmannuelle meets the Danish wife-swoppers* on the ground that it is 'trivial'.

Freaky — Loony.

Free round-the-world cruise, ski-ing holiday, etc., offered — Nasty little squirt who can get a woman only by paying for her.

Freethinking — Screws around.

Friendly	Fixed, inane smile, like a Mormon missionary.
Fun-loving / fun-seeking	Screws around.
French (ad. in)	Pretentious and pathetic — unless advertiser actually French, of course.
Gay	So outrageously camp that anyone, gay or straight, would be embarrassed to be seen with it; makes Quentin Crisp look like Burt Reynolds.
Generous	Will cough up for expensive meals, but expects enormous 'favours' in return.
Gentle	Nonetity; probably hippy.
Gentleman	Elderly buffoon.
Good life	Dirty weekends; high-stake gambling; group sex; teenaged girls; general debauchery; ie: good life.
Good natured	Tricky: could mean 'can be taken advantage of', but probably whines a lot if you do.
Gorgeous	Daffy showgirl.
Graduate	Diploma in plumbing from Rotherham Poly.
Gregarious	Has fantasies about gang-bangs.
Hairy	Man: resembling Karl Marx. Woman: resembling Groucho Marx.

Handsome — Handsome, but freaks out if you spill wine on his trousers; looks over your shoulder while he's talking to you; checks reflection in shop windows.

Heavy metal, Into — Totally deaf.

Hedonist — Glutton; possibly, a 2,000-year-old Greek.

Help! — Last ditch stand by born failure.

Hippy — Lives in squat; permanently unemployed; stoned all the time (see also 'Cycling').

Holiday companion — Sleeping bag (companion).

Homeloving — Woman: anal retentive, compulsive cleaner.
Man: slob.

Humorous — Possibly certifiably insane; knows Monty Python parrot sketch word-perfect.

Idealistic — Do please be careful. Before you know that is happening you will be bused off to a Save the Coypu rally. Your Joseph dresses will be replaced by cheap T-shirts bearing silly slogans, and the lapels of your coats will be perforated by badges; and you will be savaged by a rabid coypu.

Independent — It would be nice to believe this meant 'receiving a private income'. It generally means the same as 'Freethinking'.

Intellectual	Brooding; possibly depressive Eastern European; fun not to be with.
Interesting	About as interesting as a vacuum.
Jewish	Mother problems; but may know a good recipe for chicken soup.
Jogging, Running	Talks incessantly about cartilage trouble, Achilles tendons and running shoes; permanently exhausted; sexual activity zero.
Junoesque	Queenly; see 'Gay'.
Kind-hearted	Empty-headed.
Kindred spirit	Narcissus.
Large	Both sexes: piggish; almost unbelievably overweight. Man: great mounds of flesh spilling out of clothes, sweats profusely and smells like frying bacon. Woman: wears bell-tents, has double chins that look like an Elizabethan ruff.
Late forties	Receiving old-age pension.
Left wing	Bearded and duffel-coated; refers to all left wing politicians by their first names and all right wingers by their surnames; mutters a lot about dialectical materialism and real ale.
Lonely	Has habits so awful that they can't be legally described in an advertisement; deserves to be lonely.

Lookalike (Pamela Stephenson, Clint Eastwood, Redford, etc.)	Approximately the same colour hair; otherwise not the faintest similarity.
Looking for deep and meaningful relationship	Looking for father/mother for five quite appalling brats under the age of six.
Loves animals	House stinks of cats.
Man of the world	Suffers from incurable herpes.
Mature	Menopausal.
Model	Prostitute.
Motorcycles, Into	Leather, studs, chains, Into.
Much travelled	Long-distance trucker; if genuinely an airline pilot, see 'Man of the world'.
Music, Interested in	Several interpretations: has £50,000 laser-hologramic octophonic set-up that can kill at a mile range; has Woolworths music centre and two Barry Manilow LPs; is David Bowie.
Mystic, Occultist, etc.	Mad; involved in bizarre religious cult that advocates sex orgies, flagellation, ritual suicide, etc.
Nice	Wet, or maybe inhabiting a city on the French Riviera.
Non-camp	Despite a penchant for attending parties dressed as Carmen Miranda.
Non-effeminate gay	Tattooed, six-day beard growth,

	huge muscles, army boots and flying jacket; (chancy if female).
Non-emotional / non-heavy	See 'Freethinking'.
Non-scene gay	Once had a nasty experience with a gigantic sailor.
Occasionally moody	Invariably moody; suicidal.
Older partner, Seeks	Weird gerontophile.
Overweight / plump / Rubensesque / stocky	See 'Large'.
Personal growth, Into	Either: increased consciousness (vegetarian, left wing one-parent lesbian Zoroastrian); The Incredible Hulk; penile extension, Into.
Petite	Midget.
Presentable	Suit-owning.
Prince Charming	More like the frog.
Professional	Civil servant.
Professor	Older lecherer.
Pubs, Into	Man: talks incessantly about football and cars; fat alcoholic. Woman: outmoded dolly bird.
Quiet	Dull.
Quite attractive	Quite revolting.
Radical	On probation for assault during a demo.

Rambling, Into	See 'Country walks'; or possibly conducts rambling conversations, suffering from senile dementia.
Randy	Suffers from premature ejaculation; treats women as objects and objects as women.
Redhead	Carrothead.
Refinement, Enjoys	Provided someone else is paying.
Resilient	Victim of husband-battering.
Ritzy, chic, etc.	Tarted up like a drag queen; a bitch on wheels; even Bryan Ferry would be scared.
Romantic / tender	Woman: Pre-Raphaelite manqué; spaced out. Man: behaves like a bloody fool; moons about like a complete clot and quotes Keats.
Science-Fiction fan	Has pointed ears and green hair; says 'beam me up, Scotty' when anything goes wrong, and 'entering warp factor three' when he changes gear.
Seeks girl / guy (no specific details)	Not fussy as long as it screws.
Seeks similar	Uttery narcissistic.
Seeks solvent man / woman	Fortune hunter / gigolo.
Self-contained	Introverted to the point of being a hermit.
Sensitive	Woman: highly strung; cries a lot;

has three nervous breakdowns a year; temporarily out of asylum.
Man: poovy.

Shakespeare (advertisement quotes from) — Out of work Eng. Lit. graduate.

Sharing relationship — Screwing relationship.

Shy — Retarded.

Sincere — Clings like a leech; impossible to get rid of.

Single — Peculiar in some unspecified way.

Slightly crazy — Founder member of the Charles Manson Fan Club.

Slim — Man: gangling, roundshouldered, 6ft 6ins plus.
Woman: terminal anorexic.

Social worker — Impoverished.

Solicitor — Articled clerk in a solicitor's office; pimp.

Solitude, Into — Layabout.

Solvent — Has twelve credit cards.

Songs (quotations from in advertisement) — Ludicrous twerp.

Sophisticated — Swinger; see also 'Man of the world'.

Space, Needs — Wants to conduct seven affairs simultaneously without inter-

	ference; possibly astronaut fixation.
Sparkling personality	High as a kite on something or other; hellish bore.
Spontaneous	Erratic, unpredictable (as in 'spontaneous combustion').
Sports, Interested in	Darts; strip-poker; pinball; space invaders; group sex.
Star sign (reference to in advertisement)	Gullible nitwit.
Stockbroker	Minor clerk in stockbroking firm.
Straight-looking	Queer-acting.
Successful	At everything except personal relationships.
Talented	Makes models of the Houses of Parliament out of matchsticks.
Tall	Man: difficult one, this – either very short and lying, or exceptionally tall (over 7ft) and playing it down. Woman: resembles a stick insect.
Teacher	Broke and scruffy.
Teddy bear	The same as 'Cuddly' (Man); looks like David Bellamy, and if you're really unlucky has the same irritating voice; does Goon impressions in public.
Thai / Venezuelan / Xhosa, etc.	Doesn't speak a word of English; after free language tuition, British nationality and an easy lay.

Travelling, Keen on	Massive rent arrears.
Trendy	Looks ridiculous; wears purple lurex leotard and rainbow-coloured dreadlocks; if man, see 'Gay'.
Twenty-nine	Forty-nine.
Understanding	Real live saint sought by loser with remarkable number of problems.
Unfulfilled	Whiner.
Uninhibited	Strips off at parties.
Unpossessive	See 'Space, Needs'.
Unpredictable	May unpredictably attempt to bury a meat axe in your head.
Vibrant	Terrifying.
Virile	The same as 'Randy', but bald.
Vivacious	Freaky and volatile.
Warm	Overpowering personality; suffering from malaria.
Wild	Keep your chainsaw locked up.
Witty	Quotes Dorothy Parker and Oscar Wilde – and looks a bit like both.
Working class	And boy, doesn't he want you to know it!; rough trade.
Worldly	Travelling salesman for computer software firm; drinks and smokes to excess; looks twenty years older

than he is; see also 'Man of the world'.

Writer — Unpublished writer.

Young — (Seeking) Middle-aged man after nymphet; older woman after young stud.
(Described as) Not young.

Youthful — Old, but infantile.

Zany — Even weirder than 'Vivacious'.

There's a lot of it about.

MEDICINE

Aerobic exercises	Exercise to the brink of cardiac arrest.
Discomfort ('you may experience some discomfort')	Excruciating agony.
If symptoms persist, consult your doctor	You have misdiagnosed your illness, but your GP may be able to save you.
I think I'd better refer you to a specialist	I'm completely baffled.
It's perfectly normal	For a dead baboon.
Just a little prick	Injection that is not too painful; possibly a description of the recipient, or part of his anatomy.
Natural childbirth	And what could be more natural than a woman giving birth while naked, supported by a hairy French doctor, singing *La Marseillaise* and dropping the baby into a plastic paddling pool full of dirty, tepid salt water?
There's a lot of it about	Despite which, I haven't a clue what it is or how to treat it, so push off.
There's a new drug on the market	I am going to use you as a human guinea pig.
What we doctors call . . .	Guaranteed to put you in your place, ignoramus.

You won't feel a thing

Because you will be totally paralysed, in a coma, or dead.

PEOPLE AND PHRASES

Adorable	Child in pretty clothes, beneath which is a MONSTER.
Aristocratic	Snooty.
Assertive	Pushy.
Athletic	Narcissistic.
Bearing	Ponderousness.
Big-boned	Big all round.
Caring type of person	Interfering busybody.
Character	Fearful old bore.
Charming	Vacant, but smiles a lot.
Cosmopolitan	Mixed-racial drifter.
Creative	Involved in some undefinable, vaguely arty job.
Cute	Small and rather insignificant.
Dedication	Fanatical singlemindedness.
Delicate	Anorexic.
Dignified / distinguished	Old and ponderous.
Divine	Like 'Charming', but speaks.
Elfin	Weasel-faced girl midget.
Exotic	Coarse-featured.

Ghastly	Person or thing belonging to a lower social order.
Good friend	Person one can exploit; not to be confused with 'Just Good Friends'.
Gracious	Old, rich person.
Heavenly	Like 'Divine', but slightly less outgoing.
Human	Does not behave like an android.
Hysterical	Mildly amusing; loony.
I'd be the *last* to suggest . . .	I'd be the first to suggest . . .
I know him very well	I saw him once at a party; he doesn't know me from Adam.
I'd like to think that . . .	But as I'm not a complete moron like you, I don't.
I'll have to come back to you on that one	My total incompetence is in danger of being found out; I need more time.
I'm not racially prejudiced, but . . .	I am just about to sound off about my prejudices.
I've heard so much about you	All of it quite appalling.
I wouldn't dream of . . .	I don't need to dream, since I'm going to do it anyway.
Juicy (gossip)	Sexual.
Just Good Friends	At it hammer and tongs.

Legend (as in 'A legend in his own lifetime')	Dreadful old bore who refuses to retire with dignity.
Let's get this into perspective	Let's see this *my* way.
Let's have lunch sometime / I'll phone you	Piss off.
Let's look at / sit round the table and examine . . .	Do absolutely bugger all about . . .
Little woman	Fat wife.
Loved one	A stiff.
Loved ones	Living relatives.
Meaningful relationship	See 'Just Good Friends'.
Media person	See 'Creative'.
Multi-faceted	Person who does a bit of this and a bit of that, and maybe a bit of the other for a living.
One for the road	One more drink and there's a fair chance your body will be incorporated into the fabric of the road.
Personality (as in 'A great personality')	Ugly.
Refined	Upright.
Respect	Fear.

Striking (looks)	Cauliflower ears; broken nose; hare-lip; ugly.
This might amuse you / I've heard a marvellous story / have you heard the one about . . .?	I am about to bore you to death.
Vulnerable	Pathetic.
Willowy	See 'Delicate'.
With the greatest respect . . .	I am just about to insult you.

THE PERFORMING ARTS, TELEVISION AND RADIO

Accessible	Less esoteric than the director's other self-indulgent outpourings.
Another chance to see . . .	Fifth repeat.
Bawdy romp	Dirty movie, but in ye olde costume.
Brave (as in 'a brave excursion into New Wave music')	Tried something new, didn't work, better luck next time.
Bubbling	Featuring speed-crazed performers.
Cast of thousands	Thousands of extras; two minor 'stars'.
Catchy tune	Boring and repetitive.
Celebrity	Person who appears to have no gainful employment other than appearing on quiz programmes billed as a celebrity.
Chart smash / smash hit	Crept in at 143.
Colossal (film)	Colossal budget, most of which ended up snorted through the nostrils of the cast and crew.
Contains explicit scenes / a new experience in sensuality, etc.	Perhaps contained explicit scenes, but savagely cut by censor; go to Paris or New York if you want to see them.

Dazzling show	Sequined dancers.
Deceptively simple (song, play, etc.)	Simple.
Delicious	Containing traces of irony or black humour.
Eagerly-awaited	Excessively delayed by inefficient distribution system.
Effective (rock music)	Loud.
Epic	Film starring Charlton Heston.
Erotic	Nude women; men never entirely so.
Experimental (theatre, art, etc)	Pointless exercise in self-indulgence, with no aim or conclusion – the antithesis of a scientific experiment.
Expressive	Totally meaningless.
Fat (rock music)	Lots of bass; loud.
Fresh winds (TV weather forecast)	Bloody freezing.
Frolic	See 'Bawdy romp'.
Genial	Adjective used to describe TV 'quizmasters', vicious, aggressive ones never having proved popular.
Glittering cast	Comprising at least one British theatre knight and one Hollywood hasbeen.
Golden Age of Hollywood	Silent, out of copyright era.

Goofy / madcap / screwball / whacky / zany comedy	Noisy, manic American nonentities rushing around smashing up cars.
Hard-hitting / pulls no punches	Gratuitously violent.
Haunting theme music	Music you hadn't noticed until a TV ad repeatedly referred to it as 'haunting'.
Horrific / the most horrific film ever made	Another splatter movie.
Hospitality suite	Behind the scenes room in a TV studio where chat show guests get smashed.
Incorrigible / inimitable irrepressible	Boring egocentric old fart.
Innovative (rock music)	What used to be described as 'experimental'; cacophonous.
Introducing . . . (films)	Producer's girlfriend.
Legendary	If still alive, astonishingly decrepit old jazzer who can still list every musician on every record (or phonograph cylinder) he ever made; if dead, micro-talented rock singer who overdosed or choked to death.
Lighthearted comedy	Trite, superficial rubbish.
Lovely, The	Like 'Celebrity', but blonde.

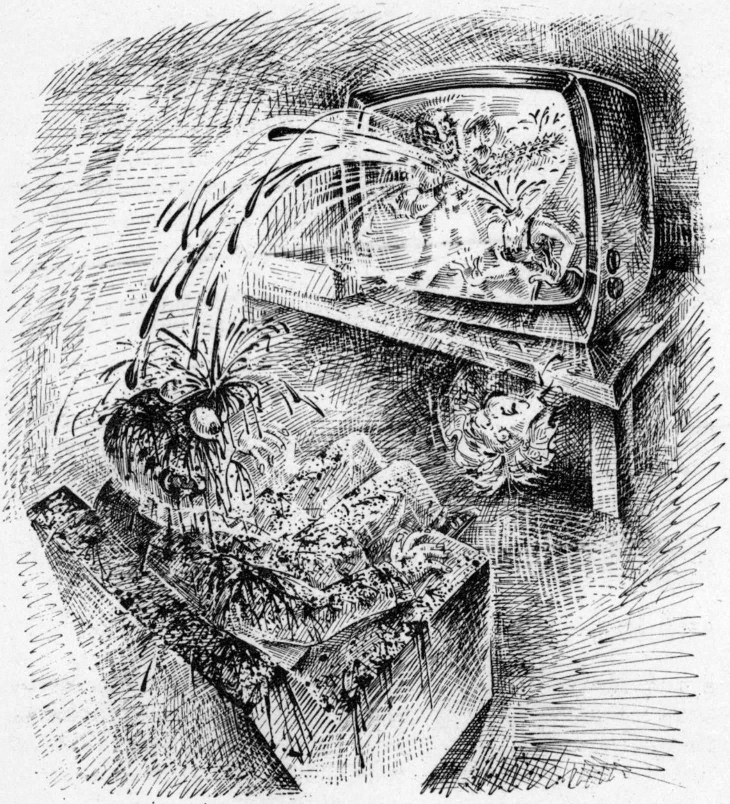

Horrific/the most horrific film ever made.

Lush Any vegetation described in a TV natural history film.

Made in black and white And therefore, curiously enough, screened in black and white.

Magnetic Attracting paying customers.

Minimal (rock music) Three chords.

Much-loved Over-exposed.

Needs no introduction Largely because he/she doesn't do much else these days except appear on shows where he/she is introduced with the phrase, 'needs no introduction'.

Occasional showers (TV weather forecast) Torrential and persistent rain.

Phone-in Cheap programme involving largely inarticulate extremist callers who say 'basically' a lot, and possibly an 'expert'.

Pithy dialogue Critic has a lisp.

Proficient debut Didn't actually fall over.

Proud (anthropological documentaries, as in 'these proud people') Surly; resentful of the intrusion of teams of German photographers.

Remix (rock music) Confusing and repetitive rehash of a minor hit single.

Resourceful (rock music) Directionless.

Rolling in the aisles	Critics pissed.
Run and run (as in 'this show will run and run')	Will close in a fortnight.
Screen classic	Film starring Humphrey Bogart.
Special	Embarrassing sequence of acts introduced by and 'starring' an emotional hasbeen who is applauded every time he/she sings the first note of a song or dances a single step; switch off if they sing 'My Way'.
Spectacular	A cross between a 'Special' and a 'Dazzling show'.
Swedish film	Porn.
Talent show	Show in which a bunch of would-be stars at least make you grateful for the fact that there are a few genuinely talented people around.
Tearjerker	Cunningly devised sentimental film in which the girl either gets her man or dies of cancer.
. . . thon	Unbelievably mindless charity show featuring unrehearsed 'celebrities' who aren't quite sure what the dickens they are doing there.
Tight (rock music)	Noisy.
Timing	That attribute alleged to have been the key to the success of a number of dead and near-dead comedians.

Tribute to (TV) — Snippets of old interviews and clips of films glued together with a hastily-written superficial biographical voice-over screened on the day of a celebrity's death.

Uncompromising (rock music) — Like it or lump it.

Unforgettable — That which you had forgotten until the ad told you it was 'unforgettable'.

Unreleased record — Technically dreadful recording that includes sounds of stoned musicians swearing and giggling.

Versatile — Performer who sings, dances and walks the tightrope — but you just can't remember his name.

Veteran — Old actor you thought was dead.

POLITICS AND INDUSTRIAL RELATIONS

Acceptable losses (military)	Acceptable to everyone except those whose lives are lost and their families.
Activist	Lefty; right wingers are noted for their total inactivity.
Aid	Handout.
Align	Bring into step with *me*.
Big business	Organizations attacked by those whom they employ.
Boss (as in 'union boss', 'company boss', etc.)	Leader of opposition group.
Candid and frank discussions	Suspicious and antagonistic exchange of pleasantries.
Charismatic	Fanatical; Hitlerian.
Collective bargaining	Pay demands coupled with threats of strikes.
Cooling-off period	Tactical reappraisal period.
Defence (budget, expenditure, etc.)	Attack.
Democratically elected representatives	Gang leaders voted in by vociferous minority.
Democratic Republic	Totalitarian dictatorship.
Derisive	Any proffered pay rise less than 300%.

Disgraceful / disgusting / filthy / foul / indecent / monstrous / obscene / revolting, etc.	Any action disapproved of by political opponents.
Emergent nation	Stone Age country.
Fraternity	Gang of opponents.
Freedom fighter	Proponent of regime one supports; see also 'Terrorist'.
Go slow	Stop.
Imperialist	Commonly used of the USA – interestingly one of the few major powers never to have had an empire.
Industrial action	Industrial inaction.
. . . ism	Variant form of communism (Marxism, Leninism, Trotskyism, etc.) or similar pseudo-belief (Conservatism, spiritualism, paganism, etc.)
Land reform	Land confiscation.
Limited nuclear war	Belief that a nuclear war in which not quite everyone is annihilated is possible.
Living wage	Minimum wage to enable wage-earner to afford basic necessities, such as a new car every year, stereo video, Bahamian holidays, etc.
Misrule (as in 'Tory misrule' 'Labour misrule')	Problems for which the opposition party has no sensible solutions.

Freedom fighter.

My Right Honourable friend	That filthy, lying, good-for-nothing cur opposite.
Pragmatic	Knowing on which side one's bread is buttered.
Privileged	People richer than the speaker.
Separate development	One-sided, i.e. white, development.
Solidarity	Affiliation with obscure overseas group.
Systems (as in 'defence systems', 'weapons systems', etc.)	Bombs.
Terrorist	Opponent of regime one supports; see also 'Freedom fighter'.
Underdeveloped	Impoverished.

THE PRESS

Actor / pop singer dies (newsvendor's placard)	Totally forgotten actor / pop singer croaks.
Agony / anguish / torment (as in 'a mother's agony')	Generally a parent waiting for news about a child who has run away, been jailed for drug offences in Turkey or got stuck in a pothole.
Anger	Someone sulking because he didn't get his own way.
Artistic	Very gay.
Attack	Criticism.
Attractive (usually followed by 'housewife' or 'mother of three')	Any female under forty.
Baron	Powerful criminal, leader of drug gang, head of newspaper group, etc.
Battle	Negotiation.
Bid	Financial offer or rescue attempt, or both.
Blast	Explosion of any magnitude from a minor gas leak to atomic bomb.
Blow	Setback, usually financial.
Blunder	Someone's said something they shouldn't.

Boycott	Apathy.
Bulgarian / Libyan	Assassin.
Bumper issue (woman's magazine)	Containing even more advertisements for sanitary towels than usual.
Campaign	Complaint voiced by more than one person.
Candid	Privacy-invading.
Carnage	Anything from genocide to the defeat of a football team.
Castle-owning baronet	Broke.
Chaos	What happens in the middle of winter when those foolish enough to drive their cars across the Pennines get stuck in snow drifts.
Charged, A man is expected to be	The police have caught the bastard; he is undoubtedly guilty, but we can't name him until he's been charged.
Clash	Argument.
Company	Female company.
Confirmed bachelor	Man who, for reasons best known to himself, has chosen not to marry; roaring pooftah.
Constant companion	Lover.
Courage	Fortitude manifested by a person who, despite Press harrassment, fails to crack up.

Craggy.

Craggy	Face like E.T.
Crippled (as in tanker)	Boat with a hole in it.
Crisis	Any event giving rise to concern among more than a handful of people.
Daring	A robbery during which 'daring' villains armed with pickaxe handles, revolvers and sawn-off shotguns have attacked two defenceless 'guards'.
Dash	Sick person taken to hospital.
Deb of the year	Experienced sort of young lady.
Debutante ball	Drugs party with bowties.
Denial (as in 'blunt denial' — or even 'Blunt denial')	Quotation made immediately prior to exposure.
Disgusting	More or less anything not approved of.
Dispute	Argument over pay.
Distinguished peer	Old fool drawing £27 a day expenses.
Drama	Event.
Drought / heatwave	Time in summer when it hasn't rained for several days.
Eccentric (especially 'eccentric peer')	Wealthy loony.

Escapade / jape / prank / stunt — Foolhardy enterprise, often undertaken by students, that doesn't actually end in anyone getting severely maimed or killed.

Exclusive — Story carried by fewer than half the nationals.

Experienced player — Old, bald player.

Explosive report — Bang! Alternatively, a report that doesn't totally whitewash all concerned.

Exposes — Summarizes information you probably already knew.

Exquisite — Old queen.

Eyewitness account — Interview with person who showed up soon afterwards.

Faceless — Rich, obscure and influential — not unlike the Press.

Fairytale — Anything involving Princess Diana.

Fear — Old people worried about rent rise, or possibly a mass-murderer on the loose.

Fiasco — Any confusion, however unimportant.

Fiend — Unpleasant kind of person.

Fighting for his life — In a coma.

Finishing school — Swiss clinic for rich junkies.

Frolic — Sporting behaviour of a sexual orientation.

Hoax.

Fun-loving	Promiscuous.
Fury	Mild concern.
Giantkillers	Football team that has narrowly defeated a supposedly better team; invariably knocked out in the next round.
Gorgeous	Thick blonde in the nude.
Heart of gold	Alleged attribute of the aged mothers of convicted criminals.
Helping police with their enquiries	Guilty.
Hoax	Misinformation paid for by Press.
Holocaust / inferno	Fire.
Hope fades (as in 'hope fades for six seamen who fell overboard in the Arctic Ocean 14 hours ago')	Only an extremely optimistic person would ever have had any hope.
Horror	Anything unpleasant.
Hubby	Husband of working class person.
Human story	Embarrassingly private story exposed by Press.
Hush-hush	Work carried out by any government department.
In-depth report	Superficial article cobbled together by a bunch of overpaid drunken hacks who ran up colossal 'research expenses' (bribes,

	Scotch, girls, etc.)
Jetsetter	Wealthy cokehead.
Kinky	Sexual activity involving gadgetry or more than two people.
Kiss 'n' tell	Filth.
Lashes out	Complains.
Live-in lovers	Both still married to other people.
Lively deb	She's discovered cocaine.
Love	Sex.
Lovechild	Bastard.
Lovenest	Squalid attic.
Lunatic / maniac	Deranged poor person (see also 'Eccentric').
Lurid	Sexually titillating.
Madness	Anything from a slightly perverse political policy to the behaviour of drivers who belt along at 90 mph in thick fog.
Member of the House of Lords	Unemployed.
Mercy (usually followed by 'dash')	See 'Dash'.
Miracle	Drugs, operations, test-tube babies, etc., conferring divinity on the medical profession.
Missus	Wife of working class man.

Naughty.

Mystery / riddle	Any story about which the Press has not acquired sufficient information.
Naughty	Feature on nighties or frilly knickers.
Night (as in 'My night of passion')	Only time when Press assumes sex occurs.
Nightmare	Worry.
Ordeal	Worry.
Orgy	Party given by young persons.
Outrageous	'Actress' who takes off her clothes in restaurants and complains when gossip columns mention it.
Perfectionist (sportsman)	Temperamental; cries if he loses.
Peril	Any event with risk element.
Petite	Any female weighing less than 10 stone.
Pill	Contraceptive pill (all other kinds of pill are now called 'drugs').
Plucky / tenacious (sportsman)	Tiny; usually Italian or Spanish.
Probe	Enquiry.
Raid / swoop	More than one police officer conducting an investigation.
Rap	Official complaint.
Revulsion	Feeling, usually coupled with

Raid/swoop.

'outrage', expressed by political spokespersons after terrorist bombings.

Royal wit	Royal twit.
Runaway bride	Fifteen-year-old.
Scandal	Official discovered on the fiddle.
Scandinavian / Swedish	Pornographic videos, magazines, etc., seized by police.
Scorcher	Temperatures of more than 70°F lasting for more than two days; also occasionally used to describe a mildly erotic film.
Sensation	½% rise in bank rate.
Serious condition	Injuries that are no laughing matter.
Sex goddess	Star of scorcher.
Shock / shocker / shocking	Journalists are unique in finding anything shocking; no-one else bats an eyelid at genocide, let alone scorchers or ½% rises in the bank rate.
Smear	Criticism, with a hint of sexual deviation.
Split	A difference of opinion.
Spokesman	Person closest to hand when journalist turned up.
Stark naked	Naked, and intending to commit some illicit act.

Starlet	Whore.
Struggle	An attempt to resolve a problem.
Student	Middle Eastern agitator.
Surprise	Rather like a 'shock', but not unpleasant – like the bank rate *not* going up ½%.
Swindle	Embezzlement of any kind, from snitching £30 from pensioners' holiday fund to £30 Million from a bank.
Teenager	Any individual aged between 10 and 25 involved in a drugs riddle, drama or orgy.
Terror	Mild alarm.
Threat	Potential termination of any service, such as a bus route.
Tired	Sozzled.
Tragedy	Anything a bit unpleasant.
Tug-of-love	Dispute between parents in which love is notably absent.
Undisclosed destination	Undisclosed to the Press because they have been a wretched nuisance.
Vice	Sex, vices such as gluttony or cruelty having been relegated to the status of bad habits.
Whizz-kid	Young tycoon, usually those involved in shady business enterprises.

Wiry (sportsman)	Small and nervy.
Wonder drug	Untested drug.
Young Eton-educated stock-broker	Young heroin addict.

PUBLIC SPEAKING

As every schoolboy knows . . .	Even though it is 50 years since I was a schoolboy.
As you all know / as Hamlet says . . . / wasn't it Tacitus who said . . .?	I am about to put you in your place.
Dear friends . . .	Peasants . . .
I'm sorry to interfere / interrupt, but . . .	I am going to push in regardless.
In my humble opinion	If said by the millionaire president of an international bank, a fairly meaningless phrase.
It should be obvious to anyone with the meanest intelligence	Listen, riffraff . . .
I've spoken for quite long enough	I am too drunk to remember what I was going to say next.
I would like to think that	However, I don't.
Let's come back to that	With a bit of luck we'll avoid coming back to it.
Of course . . .	I am crediting you with a modicum of knowledge, although I know 90% of what I am going to say will go right over your heads.
Please let me finish	And when I have, I'll do my best to prevent you from doing the same.

The man on the Clapham omnibus	Not, however, a vehicle on which I customarily travel.
The most important thing to emerge from this discussion is . . .	I shall now say it all over again.
To be perfectly frank	To be as frank as I dare without totally alienating you all.

SEX

Attractive hostesses	Prostitutes.
Be gentle with me	Shove it in.
Can I see you again?	As I didn't score this time, can I have another go?
Coffee (as in 'come up for a coffee')	Sexual intercourse.
Communicate with	Have it off with.
Corrective training / driving position / gentlemen's alterations / seats recaned / seeks unusual work / stocks and bonds for sale, etc.	Typical and quite innocuous adverts from a newsagent's window; phono numbers available on request.
Did the earth move?	Did you move? Did anything move?
Discerning (as in 'escorts for the discerning businessman')	Not too discerning – in fact, will accept anything that's offered.
Escort	Prostitute.
Exclusive club	Pick-up joint for prostitutes.
Flatmate	Consenting adult.
French lessons	With a distinct Irish accent.
Glamour (films, magazines, wear, etc.)	Porno.

High class / sophisticated (escorts, establishment, etc.)	Not too obviously riddled with venereal disease.
I find it difficult to come to terms with a long-term relationship.	I like screwing around.
I'm sure it will be OK	I have herpes.
Intimate club	Small; sexually charged.
It's never happened before	It always happens when I'm drunk.
Just look at that / those . . .	Because look is all you're ever going to get the chance to do.
Male (films, mags, etc.)	Gay.
Marital aids	Sex gadgets used mainly by people who are not married.
Massage	Masturbation.
Massage parlour	Brothel.
My God, but you're beautiful!	You are plain, but I am randy and drunk.
My wife doesn't understand me	My wife understands me perfectly.
Respect	OK, I respect you; now let's fuck.
Satisfaction guaranteed	Orgasm, by one means or another, guaranteed.

She was uncontrollable	I was scared.
She's asking for it / an easy lay / a nymphomaniac, etc.	I am indulging in all sorts of fantasies about an unattainable woman.
Singles (bar, holiday, etc.)	Oddly, used in the plural; a group of loners attempting to engage in meaningful dialogues with other 'singles'.
Stimulating (atmosphere, escorts, etc.)	Sexually arousing.
Swedish	Bleach-blonde scrubber.
Was that good for you too?	Sorry – I'd temporarily forgotten you were there.
We have a very open relationship	I screw around; she doesn't.

TRANSPORT

Courtesy (bus, phone, etc.)	Free.
Departure lounge	Waiting room.
50 mph (motorway sign)	85 mph.
For your comfort and safety	For our convenience.
Guard	Old man, the sole function of whom seems to be the object of attack by skinheads.
Incident on the line	Suicide on the line.
Lounge	Place where it is impossible to do so.
New fare structure	More expensive fare structure.
Now boarding at Gate X	You are now invited to drag yourself plus handbaggage along miles of corridors to endure a further wait in a smaller 'departure lounge'.
Opening in spring 1986 (motorway)	Unless, as a result of some entirely unforseen circumstance (such as winter) it is delayed until autumn 1989.
Points failure / frozen	Non-appearance of driver.
Reduce speed now (motorway)	Or, if you'd rather, leave it until the last moment.

Now Boarding at Gate X.

Service	Cancellation of service.
Terminal	Should mean the end of a journey, but unless you are lucky enough to live in Terminal 3 at Heathrow a 'terminal' is a stop-off point.
Unavoidable delay	Resulting from the astonishing discovery that in the middle of winter it sometimes snows.

THE EMPEROR OF THE UNITED STATES OF AMERICA AND OTHER MAGNIFICENT BRITISH ECCENTRICS
by Catherine Caufield

Wildly funny stories of over 1,000 delightfully dotty individuals who actually lived: glorious eccentrics given to dining their pets at table, conducting elaborate practical jokes, wearing odd clothes, indulging in strange phobias and leaving outrageous wills, including:

WILLIAM BUCKLAND (1784–1856) who, until he ate a bluebottle, maintained that the taste of a mole was the most repulsive he knew . . .

OSBORNE DE VERE BEAUCLERK (1875–1964), 12th Duke of St Albans, who proposed attending the 1953 Coronation with a live falcon on his wrist . . .

SIMEON ELLERTON (1694–1799) who preferred walking with a large stone on his head . . .

JOHN ALLINGTON (1795–1863) who enjoyed being carried around in an open coffin. "You see," he would explain, "I'm getting ready . . ."

'Weird, wonderful and so eccentric'
Peter Grosvenor, Daily Express

'When life seems weary, stale, and exactly the same at last Monday, this is a cheering book'
Irish Times

0 552 99007 8 £1.75

JOLLY MARSUPIAL
Down Under And Other Scenes
by Jilly Cooper

More infectious humour and witty observations from Jilly Cooper, whose latest collection of articles, originally published in *The Sunday Times* and the *Mail on Sunday*, includes a light-hearted and irreverent account of a visit to Australia, published for the first time in its entirety. Scenes nearer home, viewed with equal disrespect, include the diverse worlds of a vet's conference, fashionable charity balls, the London to Brighton run and Hen Night in Wandsworth. And, as always, Jilly Cooper is a devastating, hilarious and sometimes moving chronicler of the minutiae of family life, with some fascinating sidelights and side-swipes at the middle-class educational rat race along the way.

This new set of writings will prove once again Jilly Cooper's ability to provoke, fascinate and – above all – amuse!

0 552 12359 5 £1.75

THE CULT OF THE EXPERT
by Brian J. Ford

'Splendidly irreverent, mischievous and sardonic'
Sunday Express

The Cult of the Expert is a highly entertaining and ingenious attack on the Experts who blind us with science, confuse us with jargon, frustrate us with bureaucracy, intimidate us with superiority – and yet – precisely because they are so successful at this – have the power to appropriate huge shares of public funds and to make decisions which fundamentally affect our daily lives.

Stephen Potter delighted us with *One-Upmanship*, Parkinson coined his famous *Law*, Nancy Mitford brought us *U and Non-U*. Now Brian J. Ford has added to the English language *Fashionism* and *Nonscience*.

The Cult of the Expert is a timely and important book, for its message is that our blind subservience to the Experts is leading to the decay and destruction of our society.

0 552 12249 1 £1.50

A DIRECTORY OF DISCARDED IDEAS
by John Grant

AN ABSORBING AND HILARIOUS A-Z OF LUNACIES AND CURIOS.

Throughout history, people have got their ideas and theories wrong just as often as right. And the wrong answers are frequently more interesting . . .

In the US during 1943 there was high absenteeism among women working on the filling of fire extinguishers. It was discovered this was due to a rumour that carbon tetrachloride could make you pregnant . . .

Dr Edward Clarke warned in 1873 that education could cause a woman's uterus to shrivel . . .

A palmist, Patrick Cullen, devised a technique to take prints of female breasts to predict their owner's future. Subsequently he tested virginity by examining women's silhouettes as they stood, illuminated, behind sheets . . .

The flat earth – the hollow sun – the World Ice Theory – leeching, perpetual motion, the music of the spheres – an exhaustive search through the litterbins of the past has resulted in a rich harvest of amazing and entertaining notions.

0 552 99013 2 £1.95

OUT OF ORDER
by Frank Johnson

'Extremely funny'
Malcolm Muggeridge

'Fresh, witty, shrewd and entertaining'
Sunday Express

Award-wining columnist Frank Johnson regularly delights readers of the *Daily Telegraph* and *The Times* with his gallery reports from the Theatre of Parliament.

Since 1972, the witty and often hilarious accounts of this admired and stylist parliamentary scribe have revealed what politicians really say and do. *Out of Order* is a personal selection of highlights from a day-by-day (or blow-by-blow) chronicle of events in the Commons and outside them, in times of tedium and drama, by a man acclaimed by *The Sunday Times* as the 'funniest of the poets of the mass media.'

'No one can deflate pomposity or expose hypocrisy better than he – and his saving grace has always been that he brings his gifts to bear with a splendid impartiality'
Anthony Howard, The Listener

'Irreverent, immensely readable and always entertaining'
British Press Awards

0 552 99053 1 £2.50

Author's Note

It is obviously impossible for a book of this kind to be in any way comprehensive, and its readers will think of many other examples of similarly misleading words and phrases. The author would be grateful for any suggestions for possible inclusion in future editions. He and his publishers are much too mean to pay for them, but they will be glad to acknowledge their source. Please write to:

Russell Ash
c/o Corgi Books
Century House
61–63 Uxbridge Road
London W5 5SA